Solos, Duets, and Trios with Piano Accom

Favorite Wedding Classics

FOR PIANO ACCOMPANIMENT

MW00387406

CONTENTS

Editor: Carol Cuellar
Photography: Garry Gray

© 1992 CPP/Belwin, Inc.
All Rights Administered by WARNER BROS. PUBLICATIONS INC.
15800 N.W. 48th Avenue, Miami, FL 33014

BRIDAL CHORUS

(From the opera "Lohengrin")

RICHARD WAGNER (1813-1883)
Arranged by KEITH SNELL

Bridal Chorus – 2 – 1

F3228PAX

WEDDING MARCH
(from the "Midsummer Night's Dream")

FELIX MENDELSSHON (1809-1847)
Arranged by KEITH SNELL

Wedding March – 4 – 1
F3228PAX

6

PRINCE OF DENMARK'S MARCH

JEREMIAH CLARKE (1674-1707)
Arranged by KEITH SNELL

Prince Of Denmark's March – 4 – 1
F3228PAX

10

Prince Of Denmark's March – 4 – 3
F3228PAX

AIR
(From the "Water Music")

GEORGE F. HANDEL (1685-1759)
Arranged by KEITH SNELL

Air – 2 – 1
F3228PAX

AVE MARIA
(Based on Prelude I from "The Well-Tempered Clavier")

JOHANN SEBASTIAN BACH (1685-1750)
Arranged by KEITH SNELL

Ave Maria – 4 – 1

F3228PAX

JESU, JOY OF MAN'S DESIRING

(Chorale Prelude from Cantata No. 147)

JOHANN SEBASTIAN BACH (1685-1750)
Arranged by KEITH SNELL

LET THE TRUMPETS SOUND!
(Chorus from Cantata No. 207)

JOHANN SEBASTIAN BACH (1685-1750)
Arranged by KEITH SNELL

LA RÉJOUISSANCE
("The Rejoicing" from "Music Foer The Royal Fireworks")

GEORGE F. HANDEL (1685-1759)
Arranged by KEITH SNELL

La Réjouissance – 4 – 1
F3228PAX

28

La Réjouissance – 4 – 3
F3228PAX

MARCH
(From "Judas Maccabaeus")

GEORGE F. HANDEL (1685-1759)
Arranged by KEITH SNELL

SARABANDE

JOHANN PEZEL
Arranged by KEITH SNELL

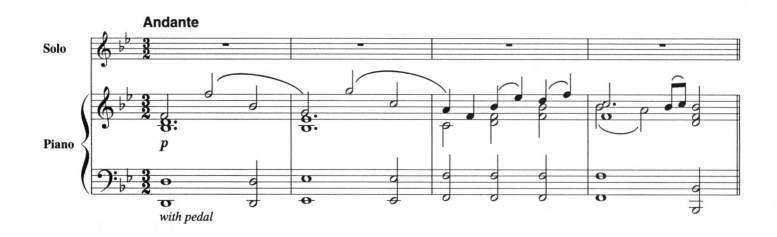

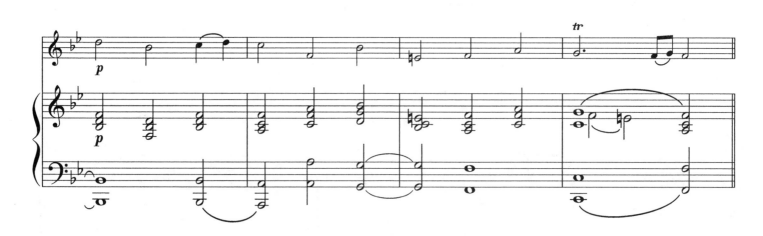

34

Sarabande – 3 – 3
F3228PAX

HORNPIPE
(From the "Water Music")

GEORGE F. HANDEL (1685-1759)
Arranged by KEITH SNELL

Hornpipe – 3 – 1
F3228PAX

36

Hornpipe – 3 – 2
F3228PAX

BIST DU BEI MIR

("If Thou Be Near" from the Anna Magdelena Notebook)

JOHANN SEBASTIAN BACH (1685-1750)
Arranged by KEITH SNELL

RONDEAU
(from "Symphonies Pour Le Roi")

JEAN JOSEPH MOURET (1682-1738)
Arranged by KEITH SNELL

Moderato

Rondeau – 4 – 1
F3228PAX

42

TRUMPET TUNE

HENRY PURCELL (1659-1695)
Arranged by KEITH SNELL

F3228PAX

PRELUDE
(From "Te Deum")

MARK-ANTOINE CHARPENTIER (1634-1704)
Arranged by KEITH SNELL